Book 5:
Later Adventures with

Clarissa and Gregory

Written and Illustrated by
Nadine Redfield

ISBN: 978-1-958407-32-5 (hardback)

ISBN: 978-1-958407-33-2 (soft cover)

WWW.ELMGROVEPUBLISHING.COM
San Antonio, Texas
Book design by: designpanache

Later Adventures with

Clarissa and Gregory

Dedicated to the memory of my dear brother,
Paul Gregory, who lived these adventures with me.

Contents

Clarissa and Gregory.
Clayton, Michigan, 1929

Meet Clarissa and Gregory

Clarissa and Gregory are real children, a brother and sister who lived in America a long time ago, long before there were cell phones or computers or even television.

They had lots of adventures together!

Some of their adventures are very funny. And some of them are very scary!

When Gregory grew up, he worked for National Cash Register. Clarissa worked as a seamstress, but she was an artist who also liked to write, and many years later, she wrote this series of books about growing up in rural Michigan in the 1920s and '30s!

Clarissa and Gregory's father, George, was the youngest of 6 children; he owned and operated a sawmill with his steam engine (often mentioned in the stories!).

A pencil drawing of George, later in his life, by Clarissa

Later Adventures with

Clarissa
and Gregory

Gregory Falls into the Icy Creek

It was that time of year again. Every March, Daddy would make maple syrup at the Sugar Bush deep in the woods. Mama told Clarissa and Gregory to go to the Sugar Bush after school to help Daddy because she wouldn't be home. She would be at the Ladies' Aide Meeting at Grandmother's house.

Once a month the ladies at the church met at one of the lady's homes to do work for a missionary whose name was Harriet Skimp. Harriet lived in Africa and wrote to the church once a month telling them what she needed. Sometimes she needed baby clothes or a quilt. The ladies kept busy providing for the needs of her people. Mama even sent some of her tomato seeds to plant in a garden in Africa.

After school Clarissa and Gregory stopped at their house to drop off their lunch boxes and grab a cookie to eat on the way. They walked on the paths through the woods, feeling grown up to be on their own and to have their parents trust them. They threw snowballs at each other and chased rabbits. Gregory threw snowballs at the squirrels but he never hit one. They stopped to drink some nice cold sap from the pails hanging from the maple trees.

Gregory pointed to the building at the bottom of the hill. "I'll race you to the Sugar Bush," he told his sister. Steam was coming out the cubicle on the top of the building.

"OK, but you always win because you are bigger than I am," Clarissa complained.

"Hi, Daddy!" the children echoed.

"I'll be ready to leave early tonight because the syrup will be finished soon. I didn't have that much sap to boil. Uncle Ray went to town and didn't gather up any sap today," Daddy told them.

The children helped by gathering wood for Daddy's steam engine. The wood was used to burn in the engine that made steam to boil the sap that made maple syrup. Daddy gave them samples of the hot maple syrup to taste.

"I think you can start home now. Mother will be home soon and I'll finish up here. I'll be along soon."

"Let's go home through the meadow and cross the creek on the plank," Gregory suggested.

"OK, but this time don't fall in the creek when we walk across the plank," Clarissa warned her brother.

Over the fence the children saw the creek full of water from all the snow that had thawed. The large wooden plank was still there. It was used as a bridge to cross over the water.

"I'll go first," Clarissa said.

Just as she was almost ready to step off the plank she heard a splash. She turned around just in time to watch Gregory's dark green stock-

ing cap appear from under the water.

"Gregory you did it again. You will catch your death of cold if we don't get you home and out of those wet clothes," Clarissa warned her brother.

"Yes, I know," grumbled Gregory as the children walked down to the basement where the kitchen was.

"I'll start a fire in the cook stove and heat some more water. A tub of hot water will warm you up," Clarissa said feeling all grown up.

Mama and Daddy appeared while Gregory was soaking in a tub of hot water. Clarissa hung up all of Gregory's wet clothes to dry.

"What happened?" Mama inquired looking at Gregory in the tub.

"Gregory fell in the creek again, Mama," Clarissa told her.

"You did the right thing to get out of those wet clothes and into a tub of hot water," Mama complimented the children. She didn't even scold them.

Clarissa was proud that she had taken such good care of her brother because he was always taking care of her. It was good to be the care-giver this time. She wondered why Gregory fell in the creek when she didn't have any trouble walking across on the plank.

"Gregory, why do you always fall in the creek? I can walk on the narrow plank without falling in—why can't you?"

"I was trying to turn somersaults on the plank."

"No wonder you fell in!" Clarissa answered.

And everyone had a good laugh.

Clarissa Learns to Ice-Skate

Clarissa listened to Daddy tell her how he ice-skated when he was a boy. He showed her the old rusty ice skates he used to skate on. The skates clamped onto your shoes.

The old skates were much too big to fit Clarissa's feet. She thought that someday her feet would grow large enough to fit the old skates. Then she could learn to ice skate like her daddy.

"I hope I can learn to ice-skate someday," Clarissa told him eagerly.

"Sonja Henie became the gold medal Olympic champion figure skater. Here is a picture of her in the paper," Daddy showed her pictures of Sonja Henie skating in beautiful costumes.

All this made Clarissa want to learn to ice-skate even more. Every year Clarissa looked at the old skates in the basement. One year she looked at the skates, and she thought they would fit if she adjusted them to the smallest size.

Clarissa cleaned up the old skates and went out to Daddy's workshop and oiled the skates really well. She was able to move the adjustable parts to fit her shoes, and then she moved the clamp to fasten them on. Now she had to wait for a pond to freeze over with ice strong enough to skate on.

"Daddy, look at the pond in our back yard between the three large maple trees. We have never had a pond out there before. Would the ice be strong enough to skate on?" asked Clarissa eagerly, thinking of the miracle that had happened.

"This is Saturday, and by tomorrow the ice should be strong enough to skate on," Daddy told her.

"Daddy, your old skates fit me now that I adjusted them to the smallest size. Tomorrow after church and dinner I am going to learn to ice-skate with your old skates. I have a pond of my very own right in our back yard," Clarissa announced.

"You had better tie a pillow on your behind because you will fall quite a few times before you learn to ice-skate," Daddy told her.

"I can bring out a chair to hold on so that I can keep from falling," Clarissa told him.

Once church was over and dinner was finished, Clarissa gathered up the old skates, an old chair, a pillow, then put on her warm coat, mittens and hat.

"I can sit on the chair to put the skates on. We have never had a pond before in our back yard so close to the house," Clarissa thought to herself.

"Now I have the skates on and the pillow tied on my behind, let's see if I can stand up on them," Clarissa wondered, pulling up and standing on her wobbling feet.

"Daddy is right, my ankles sure are wobbly," she thought turning

the chair around so she could hang on to it.

Soon she was able to push the chair ahead and walk behind it. She leaned forward to keep her balance. Then she learned to turn her skate sideways to push then glide on the other wobbly foot.

"This is fun, and I don't need this pillow anymore," she said throwing the pillow into the chair.

The three old maple trees made an umbrella overhead. Clarissa felt all enveloped in her own little wonderland.

"What a wonderful little pond God made just for me to learn to skate on. Thank you Lord for this beautiful pond," Clarissa thought gratefully.

She skated around the pond a few times when Gregory appeared.

"Look, Gregory—I am skating!"

"Try skating without the chair, Clarissa," Gregory suggested.

"OK, I'll try," Clarissa said pushing the chair aside with her wobbly foot.

"That's good Clarissa. Now that you know how to skate we can go

to a larger pond or lake and skate," Gregory told her.

"That will be fun! I will save up and buy some shoe skates," Clarissa told him.

"This is such a beautiful day, I'll remember it forever—and I never fell once!" Clarissa smiled.

The funny thing was that the pond only appeared that one time, and never appeared again!

A May Basket for Daddy's Birthday

It was May 11th, and a beautiful spring day in lower Michigan for Daddy's birthday. Clarissa and Gregory hurried home from school—they had lots of work to do to get ready for Daddy's surprise. They had made a May basket at school. It was made out of blue construction paper with stripes cut in the center part, and the ends were pasted together, a handle was pasted at the top then a round circle was pasted at the bottom. The basket puffed out at the center when placed on a table.

The children had learned at Sunday school that "It is more blessed to give than to receive."

"This is going to be so much fun, and Daddy will be so surprised," Clarissa told her brother.

"We'll go into the woods and pick the flowers first before Daddy gets home and then you can wrap his gifts," Gregory suggested.

"We can't forget to pick a trillium (wild lilies). They are so beautiful. I hope we can find some today."

"I know where some are growing. I saw some the other day in the woods. Daddy and I were looking at some trees to cut down. Come on, let's hurry."

"Mama said she had saved some popcorn from last night to put in the top the basket," Clarissa added, running to keep up with Gregory.

The children found some spring beauties right away. They are little white flowers, and there were lots of them. Then they found some purple and white violets, some adder tongues, and some Dutchmen's breeches. The boy flowers are plain but the girl flowers have ruffles on the legs to make them fancy.

"It is time to look for a trillium. I think they are over here by this big tree. Remember we can only pick one flower each time we go into the woods," Gregory advised.

"Yes, I know. If we pick all of them they won't go to seed and we won't have any flowers next year," Clarissa told him.

"Here they are, right where I saw them last week," Gregory pointed to the flowers.

"These have purple edges on them! I have never seen any with purple edges on them before. I do wish we could pick more than one," Clarissa said.

"On the way home we'll see if we can find a May apple along the road. The large leaf is like an umbrella to go over the top of the flowers."

"I like the way they smell," Gregory added.

"I wish we could find a Jack-in-the-pulpit. They look like a preacher behind a pulpit preaching a sermon," Clarissa added.

"It is too early for them—and we have enough flowers. Let's get home before Daddy gets back."

"Oh, these are pretty," Mama told them. "I'll put them in water so they won't wilt.

"OK," the children echoed in unison.

"Here are the gifts and card you ordered: the bitter sweet chocolate bar, and the large marking crayon for Daddy to mark on the end of the logs. I added some red bandana handkerchiefs.

Here is your change that I didn't use. You children bought the gifts with your own money. Daddy always carries a red or blue handkerchief you know. Take this wrapping paper, and some string to wrap the gifts. If you wrap them in your room, Clarissa, Daddy won't see you if he gets home before you are through," Mama told them.

"OK," Clarissa said, gathering the things she would need, and heading for her room. She ran back and grabbed some scissors.

"You don't have my good sewing scissors do you? You know not to cut paper with my good scissors, don't you," Mama told her.

"Yes, Mama I know," Clarissa told her.

"Are you through, yet?" Gregory asked. "I have the popcorn to put on the top, over the gifts."

"Yes, they are ready. Daddy will be so surprised. Mama baked him a cake today so we can have some after we give him his May basket. We can hide the basket under my bed so he won't see it," Clarissa told him.

The children hurried through dinner almost too excited to eat. When Daddy wasn't looking they grabbed the flowers and ran to Clarissa's room to put them on the top of the May basket. They ran out the front door, and laid the basket by the door.

"May Basket!" the children yelled to the top of there lungs. They ran and hid behind some trees.

Daddy came to the door and picked up the May basket and his Happy Birthday card.

"I do declare! I had forgotten it was my birthday!" Daddy exclaimed.

"Now don't run too fast to catch the children. You're not as young as you used to be, you know!" Mama advised.

Soon, Daddy found the children and chased them until he tagged them.

"Happy Birthday, Daddy! Mama baked you a cake. Let's go inside and have some cake," the children echoed.

Daddy opened his presents and took a bite out of his bitter sweet chocolate bar, then wrapped it back up.

"This will last me a long time, and I did need a new marker. I can always use new handkerchiefs. This is the best birthday I ever had. Thank you," Daddy told everyone as he ate his birthday cake.

The children looked at each other, "It really is more blessed to give than receive."

*   *   *

It was a tradition, each May, to decorate a box or basket and fill it with small gifts, candy and popcorn, then put flowers on the top.

The filled basket would then be taken to a friend, neighbor or relative's front door. After calling out "May Basket!" the giver would run and hide! The surprised recipient didn't know who had hung the basket, and had to find them, then chase and tag each one. After everyone was tagged they would all go inside and have refreshments. It was lots of fun!

At the end of the book you can find out how to make our own May Basket with construction paper, scissors and glue!

A Dare to Draw

It was a Sunday afternoon after church, and Uncle Ray had come for dinner at Clarissa's house. His wife, Aunt Anna, was out of town and wasn't there to cook dinner for him. Dinner was over and Mama, Daddy, Uncle Ray and Clarissa were sitting around the living room reading the Sunday paper. Clarissa was reading the funnies.

"I bet you can't draw O'Henry," Uncle Ray dared Clarissa.

"I'll try, and see if I can," Clarissa told him looking for a pencil and paper.

She sat down and started to draw. Sure enough, the drawing looked just like O'Henry.

"There, I did it," Clarissa announced, holding up her drawing.

"I do declare. It looks exactly like O'Henry," Uncle Ray exclaimed, rather surprised.

"Now let's see if you can draw a person that someone else hasn't drawn.

"OK, I'll see if I can draw Daddy. Hold still now, and I'll see if I can draw a picture of you," Clarissa told her father.

Clarissa sat down by Daddy and started to draw. Pretty soon she had a portrait drawing of her father. "It is black and white so I can't show Daddy's bright blue eyes," Clarissa said.

"Here it is," Clarissa held up the drawing.

Uncle Ray was surprised that the picture looked like Clarissa's father.

"I didn't know you could draw so well, Clarissa," Uncle Ray told her as he held up the picture for Daddy and Mama to see.

"I didn't know I could draw either," Clarissa explained more surprised than anyone.

That night Clarissa had a dream. She remembered seeing a picture in a magazine of a lady standing in front of an easel painting. In her dream it was Clarissa standing in front of an easel painting. She was so happy.

"This is why God created me so I could paint beautiful pictures," she thought.

Many years later her dream came true. She stood in front of her own easel and painted beautiful pictures.

The End

How to Make a May Basket

Use a sheet of sturdy construction paper in the color of your choice. Almost any size will work but it shouldn't be less than 8.5" x 11" (for a small basket). Make sure a grown-up helps you with the scissors!

1. *Fold the sheet of paper lengthwise and cut slits, as shown, about half an inch apart. Be careful not to cut all the way to the end!*

2. *Unfold the paper and bring the edges together, so that the two end strips overlap. Glue or staple the two end strips together and set aside to dry.*

3. *This is VERY important! Draw a circle around the end of the basket — ADD HALF AN INCH all the way around for tabs, then cut it out.*

4. *Fold the tabs and glue them to the bottom of the basket. Set aside to dry.*

5. *Cut a strip of paper from the sheet of construction paper for the handle. Glue or staple both ends to the top and let the glue dry thoroughly.*

6. *Fill the basket with goodies and decorate the top with flowers!*

1. Fold paper in half lengthwise.

Cut slits half an inch apart.

2.

Glue overlapped edges together to make a circular tube shape.

3.

Draw circle using the end of the basket.

Add half-inch tabs all the way around and fold.

4.

Glue tabs around basket to form a sturdy base.

5.

Cut a strip of paper at least one-inch wide for the handle and glue both ends across the top.

6. Your completed May Basket is ready to fill with exciting goodies!